To:

From:

Message:

Published by Christian Art Publishers
PostNet Suite # 132, Private Bag X3706, Three Rivers, 1935, South Africa

First edition 2025

Designed by Christian Art Publishers
Cover designed by Christian Art Publishers
Images used under license from Shutterstock.com

Printed in China

ISBN 978-0-638-00428-1

25 26 27 28 29 30 31 32 33 34 – 10 9 8 7 6 5 4 3 2 1

Grateful and Blessed

Christian Art
PUBLISHERS

Give us a thankful sense of the
blessings in which we live,
of the many *comforts* of our lot;
that we may not deserve to lose
them by discontent or indifference...
Hear us, *almighty God*
for His sake who has redeemed us,
and taught us thus to pray. Amen.

JANE AUSTEN

Introduction

What is gratitude?

Gratitude can be defined as the quality of being thankful and the readiness to show appreciation for kindness received. However, for the believer, gratitude goes beyond a mere feeling; it involves a deliberate choice to express thankfulness and to repay kindness despite how we feel.

Thus, gratitude is a choice—a choice to live in such a way that it reflects our relationship with God, who calls us to live lives of constant thankfulness. Although this is not always easy, by developing a habit of gratitude through intentional practice, it is possible.

Grateful & Blessed—A Guided Gratitude Journal is designed to help you develop a habit of gratitude in every area of your life. Divided into 20 themes, the inspirational quotes, Bible promises, journaling prompts, and gratitude challenges in this journal will encourage deep reflection and meditation on the blessings and grace God has bestowed on you. As Psalm 107:1 (NIV) says, "Give thanks to the LORD, for He is good; His love endures forever."

This guided gratitude journal will help you cultivate a mindset of appreciation and foster a habit of gratitude, focusing on the goodness and everlasting love of God in every aspect of your life.

1 God's Unfailing Love

God proved His love on the Cross. When Christ hung, and bled, and died, it was God saying to the world, "I love you."

BILLY GRAHAM

God, who needs nothing, loves into existence wholly superfluous creatures in order that He may love and perfect them.

C. S. LEWIS

Nothing binds me to the Lord like a strong belief in His changeless love.

CHARLES SPURGEON

God and love are synonymous. Love is not an attribute of God, it is God; whatever God is, love is.

OSWALD CHAMBERS

People's love for us may change, depending on what we do or don't do to please them. But God's does not—it's everlasting.

STORMIE OMARTIAN

Reflect on the ways God's love has been tangible in your life this week.

How can you trust that God has a plan for you?

Remember a time when God's presence was near and you experienced Him in a fresh way. Reflect on how His presence impacted your life and what it meant to you.

What are you most thankful for about your relationship with God?

Promises from God's Word

Give thanks to the LORD, for He is good; His love endures forever.

PSALM 107:1 NIV

For I am convinced that neither death nor life, neither angels nor demons, neither the present nor the future, nor any powers, neither height nor depth, nor anything else in all creation, will be able to separate us from the love of God that is in Christ Jesus our Lord.

ROMANS 8:38–39 NIV

This is how God showed His love among us: He sent His one and only Son into the world that we might live through Him. This is love: not that we loved God, but that He loved us and sent His Son as an atoning sacrifice for our sins.

1 JOHN 4:9–10 NIV

"For the mountains shall depart and the hills be removed, but My kindness shall not depart from you, nor shall My covenant of peace be removed," says the LORD, who has mercy on you.

ISAIAH 54:10 NKJV

"Greater love has no one than this: to lay down one's life for one's friends."

JOHN 15:13 NIV

Give thanks
TO THE LORD,
FOR HE IS GOOD.
His love
ENDURES
FOREVER.
PSALM 136:1 NIV

List three ways to express gratitude for God's unfailing love in your daily life.

Write down the Scripture verse that best reminds you of God's unfailing love for you.

How does knowing that God's love for you is unconditional and eternal change the way you live?

Prayer Time

Read Jeremiah 31:3 and write a prayer of thanks for God's unfailing love.

Gratitude Challenge

For the next week, set aside a few minutes each day to write a note of gratitude to God for specific ways His love has been evident in your life that day.

2

Answered Prayers

Praise should always follow answered prayer, just like the mist of earth's gratitude rises when the sun of heaven's love warms the ground. Has the Lord been gracious to you and inclined His ear to the voice of your supplication? Then praise Him as long as you live.

CHARLES SPURGEON

Answered prayer is the interchange of love between the Father and His child.

ANDREW MURRAY

More tears are shed over answered prayers than unanswered ones.

MOTHER TERESA

God answers our prayers not because we are good, but because He is good.

A. W. TOZER

God answers the prayer we ought to have made rather than the prayer we did make.

J. I. PACKER

There is nothing meritorious in our prayers...whenever God hears them, it is in exercise of His free goodness.

JOHN CALVIN

Describe a time when prayer changed your life. Why are you grateful for this moment?

Reflect on any lessons you learned during the process of waiting or receiving the answer to your prayer.

Reflect on the lessons God taught you by saying no to a prayer request.

Can you list 3 instances in the Bible where God answered someone's prayer of faith spectacularly?

Promises from God's Word

This is the confidence that we have in Him, that if we ask anything according to His will, He hears us. And if we know that He hears us, whatever we ask, we know that we have the petitions that we have asked of Him.

1 JOHN 5:14–15 NKJV

I love the LORD, because He has heard my voice and my pleas for mercy. Because He inclined His ear to me, therefore I will call on Him as long as I live.

PSALM 116:1–2 ESV

"Keep on asking, and you will receive what you ask for. Keep on seeking, and you will find. Keep on knocking, and the door will be opened to you. For everyone who asks, receives. Everyone who seeks, finds. And to everyone who knocks, the door will be opened."

MATTHEW 7:7–8 NLT

I prayed to the LORD, and He answered me.

PSALM 34:4 NLT

Do not be anxious about anything, but in every situation, by prayer and petition, with thanksgiving, present your requests to God. And the peace of God, which transcends all understanding, will guard your hearts and your minds in Christ Jesus.

PHILIPPIANS 4:6–7 NIV

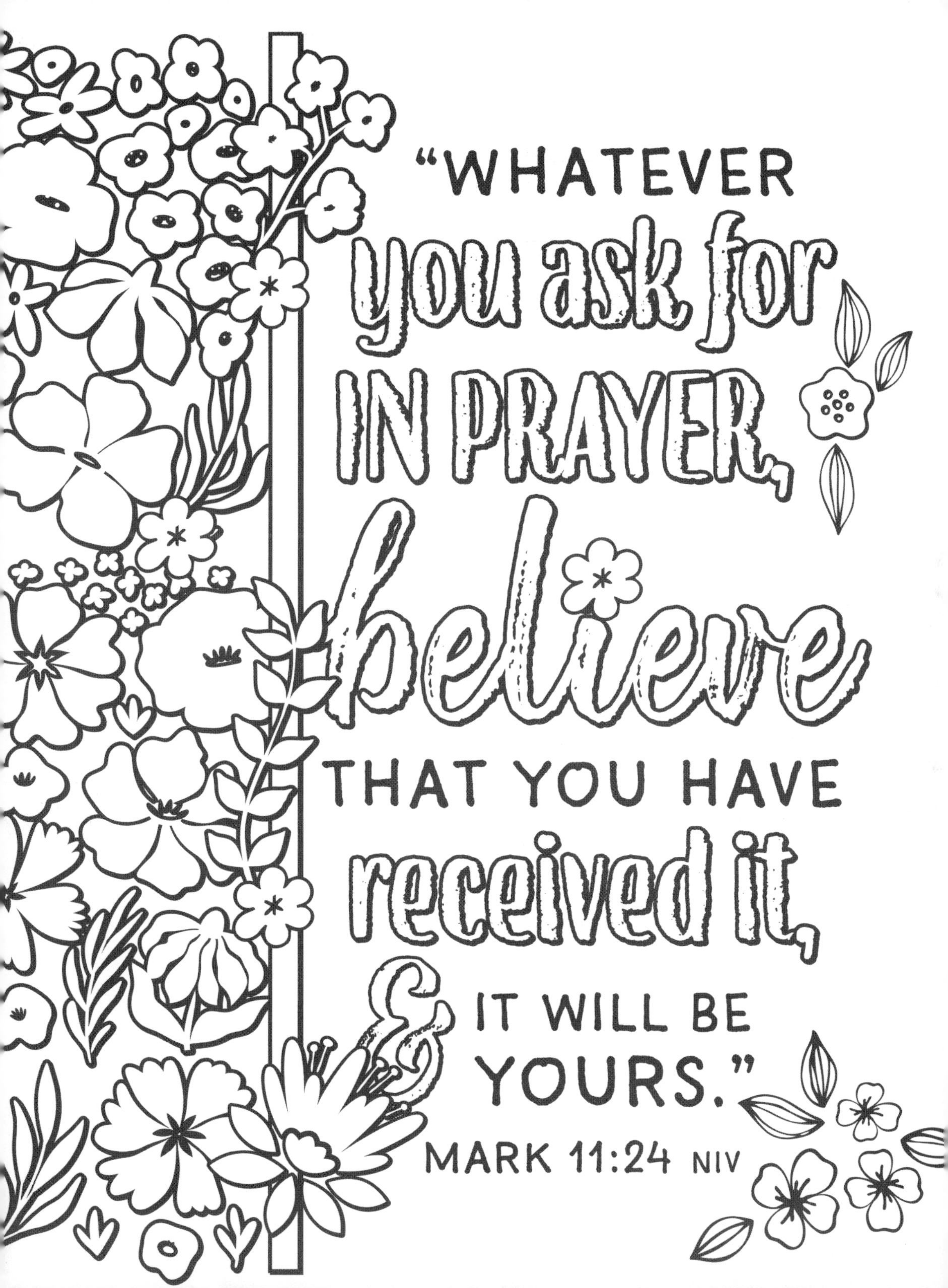
"WHATEVER
you ask for
IN PRAYER,
believe
THAT YOU HAVE
received it,
& IT WILL BE
YOURS."
MARK 11:24 NIV

List 5 of your prayers God has answered and how you expressed your gratitude.

How have you seen God work in the lives of others through your prayers for them?

Recall one instance where God's answer to your prayer exceeded your expectations.

Prayer Time

Lord Jesus,

In Scripture, You say that if we ask anything according to Your will, You hear us. If we believe we will receive what we ask for, it will be ours. Thank You, Lord, for all the prayers You have answered in the past and those You will answer in the future.

However, sometimes I don't receive a speedy answer or the answer I desire. Please grant me the patience to wait for You, as well as the peace and acceptance when I receive a different answer than I expected.

Thank You for the Holy Spirit who intercedes for me when I don't know what words to pray. You are indeed all-knowing and almighty. Amen.

Gratitude Challenge

Start a prayer journal or a prayer jar where you write down answered prayers. Every time God answers one of your prayers, add it to the journal or jar. Review these as a reminder of His faithfulness and express thanks each time you reflect on the answers.

3

The Beauty of God's Creation

The majesty of God is magnified when we see Him through the lens of creation *ex nihilo* (out of nothing).

JOHN PIPER

Creation is the canvas on which God has painted His character.

UNKNOWN

Among the many acts of gratitude we owe to God, it may be accounted one to study and contemplate the perfections and beauties of His work of creation. Every new discovery must necessarily raise in us a fresh sense of the greatness, wisdom, and power of God.

JONATHAN EDWARDS

Creation is a constant reminder that God is the author of all things.

R. C. SPROUL

Look up on a starry night, and you will see the majesty and power of an infinite Creator.

BILLY GRAHAM

How can you see the beauty of God's creation in the smallest details of the world, like the intricate patterns in a leaf or the simple sound of rain? How do these moments speak of His care and attentiveness?

What do you love most about each season of the year?

Where is your favorite place in nature and why?

Describe a time in nature when you felt God's presence.

Promises from God's Word

When I consider Your heavens, the work of Your fingers, the moon and the stars, which You have set in place, what is mankind that You are mindful of them, human beings that You care for them?

PSALM 8:3–4 NIV

For ever since the world was created, people have seen the earth and sky. Through everything God made, they can clearly see His invisible qualities—His eternal power and divine nature. So they have no excuse for not knowing God.

ROMANS 1:20 NLT

Look up into the heavens. Who created all the stars? He brings them out like an army, one after another, calling each by its name. Because of His great power and incomparable strength, not a single one is missing.

ISAIAH 40:26 NLT

"Worthy are You, our Lord and God, to receive glory and honor and power, for You created all things, and by Your will they existed and were created."

REVELATION 4:11 ESV

The LORD merely spoke, and the heavens were created. He breathed the word, and all the stars were born. He assigned the sea its boundaries and locked the oceans in vast reservoirs. Let the whole world fear the LORD, and let everyone stand in awe of Him. For when He spoke, the world began! It appeared at His command.

PSALM 33:6–9 NLT

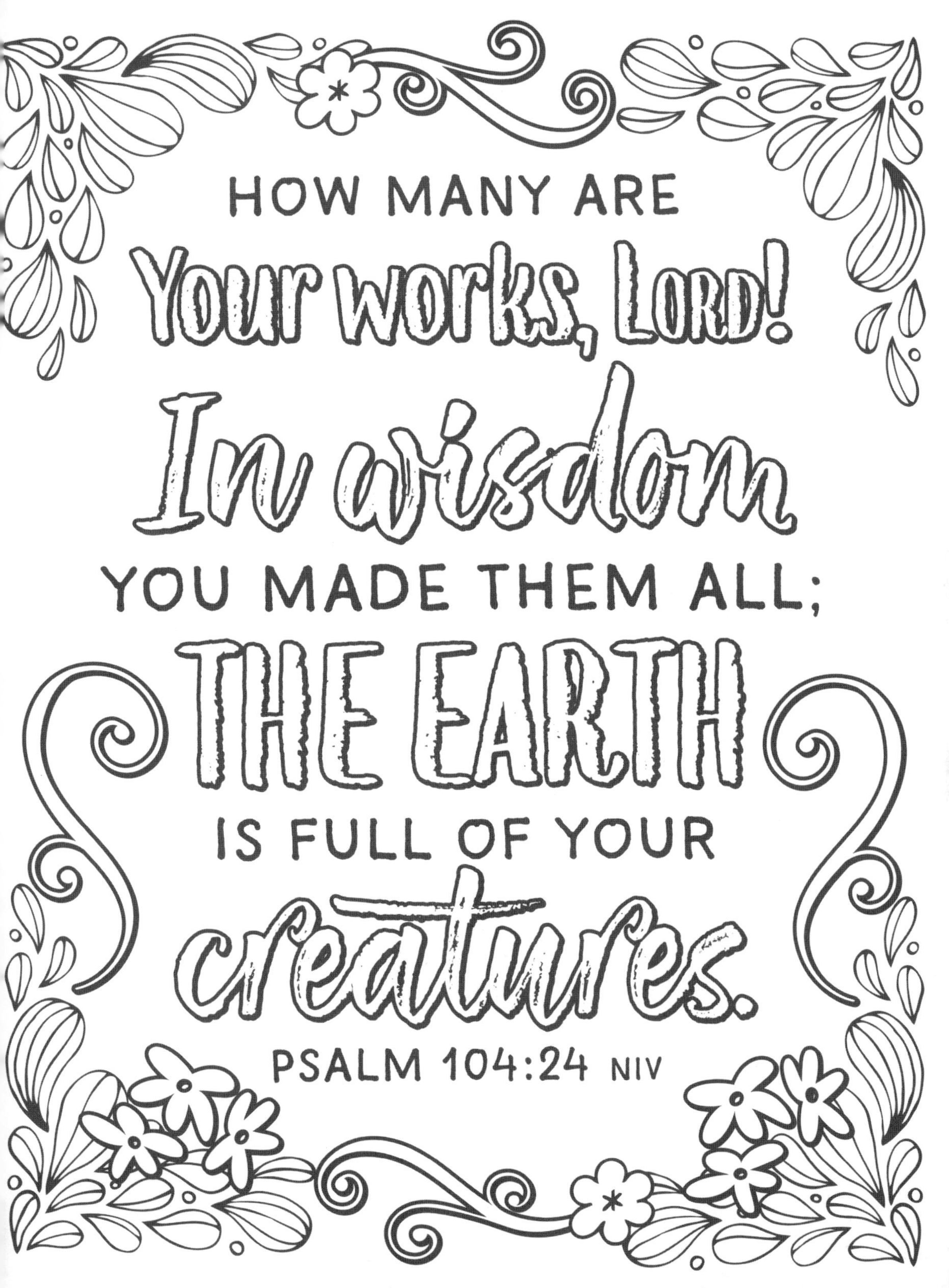
HOW MANY ARE
Your works, LORD!
In wisdom
YOU MADE THEM ALL;
THE EARTH
IS FULL OF YOUR
creatures.
PSALM 104:24 NIV

What do you consider the heavenly Father's greatest creation and why?

What aspects of nature inspire awe in your heart?

List your favorite...

Animal

Flower

Bird

Season

Place in nature

Prayer Time

God created the world in a variety of vibrant shades and colors, shapes and sizes. Write a prayer to thank God for His beautiful creation.

Gratitude Challenge

For 7 days, take one photograph a day of anything in nature that you find beautiful or inspiring. Share it on your social media platforms, stating why you are thankful for God's wonderful creation.

Joy in the Lord

Joy is not gush; Joy is not jolliness. Joy is simply perfect acquiescence in God's will, because the soul delights itself in God Himself.

BILLY GRAHAM

Joy does not simply happen to us. We have to choose joy and keep choosing it every day.

HENRI NOUWEN

An hour spent in the presence of God brings the purest joy known to man.

E. STANLEY JONES

If the Lord is your joy, your joy will never dry up.

CHARLES SPURGEON

The joy of the Lord is your strength and the person of Christ is your unassailable joy—and the battle for joy is nothing less than fighting the good fight of faith.

ANN VOSKAMP

Reflect on the difference between happiness and joy. What makes you happy, and what brings you joy?

What non-tangible joy can you appreciate today? (a smile, hug, etc.)

Is there a time in your life when you felt filled with the joy of the Lord? Reflect on that experience as you thank God for the complete satisfaction in Him.

Why do you think joy is a fruit of the Spirit (Gal. 5:22–23)?

Promises from God's Word

Though you have not seen Him, you love Him; and even though you do not see Him now, you believe in Him and are filled with an inexpressible and glorious joy, for you are receiving the end result of your faith, the salvation of your souls.

1 PETER 1:8–9 NIV

May the God of hope fill you with all joy and peace as you trust in Him, so that you may overflow with hope by the power of the Holy Spirit.

ROMANS 15:13 NIV

You make known to me the path of life; You will fill me with joy in Your presence, with eternal pleasures at Your right hand.

PSALM 16:11 NIV

I will rejoice in the LORD, I will be joyful in God my Savior.

HABAKKUK 3:18 NIV

Always be full of joy in the Lord. I say it again—rejoice!

PHILIPPIANS 4:4 NLT

MY soul WILL
rejoice
IN THE LORD
and delight
IN HIS
salvation.
PSALM 35:9 NIV

List 5 things that make you happy

List 5 things that make you sad

Reflect on the joy that comes from knowing God and how it has sustained you.

How has God helped you choose joy in a time of hardship? Reflect on the experience.

Prayer Time

Lord,

Thank You for the overflowing joy that comes from walking in Your path and trusting in Your promises. We are grateful for Your love and the joy it brings, now and forevermore.

In Jesus' name, Amen.

Gratitude Challenge

Each night before bed, take a moment to reflect on the day. List 3 things that brought you joy and that you are grateful for. Focus on the positive aspects of your day.

5

God's Faithfulness

Trust God's hold on you more than your hold on God. His faithfulness does not depend on yours. His performance is not predicated on yours. His love is not contingent on your own. Your candle may flicker, but it will not expire.

MAX LUCADO

Our God and Father is the same faithful God that He ever was—as willing as ever to prove Himself the living God, in our day as formerly, to all who put their trust in Him.

GEORGE MÜLLER

God is faithful; and that trumps all our problems, tears, tragedies, and the very prospect of death itself.

DAVID JEREMIAH

The glory of God's faithfulness is that no sin of ours has ever made Him unfaithful.

CHARLES SPURGEON

Remembering God's unceasing care for you reminds you that He will carry you through every situation in life, no matter how bad.

ELIZABETH GEORGE

What worship songs help you praise the Lord and remind you of God's faithfulness?

Reflect on how you experienced God's faithfulness in a time you followed His plan even though you didn't understand or see the way.

How can you show your gratitude for God's faithfulness in your daily life?

In what ways can you demonstrate faithfulness to God in return for His faithfulness to you?

Promises from God's Word

LORD, You are my God; I will exalt You and praise Your name, for in perfect faithfulness You have done wonderful things, things planned long ago.

ISAIAH 25:1 NIV

Let us hold fast the confession of our hope without wavering, for He who promised is faithful.

HEBREWS 10:23 NKJV

God will do this, for He is faithful to do what He says, and He has invited you into partnership with His Son, Jesus Christ our Lord.

1 CORINTHIANS 1:9 NLT

But the Lord is faithful, who will establish you and guard you from the evil one.

2 THESSALONIANS 3:3 NKJV

Know therefore that the LORD your God is God; He is the faithful God, keeping His covenant of love to a thousand generations of those who love Him and keep His commandments.

DEUTERONOMY 7:9 NIV

For the Lord is
GOOD and his
love endures
forever;
HIS FAITHFULNESS
continues through
all generations.
Psalm 100:5 NIV

In what areas of your life do you struggle to trust in God's faithfulness?

God's faithfulness is unwavering and not influenced by what we do. How does that make you feel?

What Scripture verse best reminds you of God's unfailing love for you?

Prayer Time

Write a prayer of thanksgiving for God's love and faithfulness.

Gratitude Challenge

Write down your favorite Scripture verse reminding you of God's faithfulness on a piece of paper and share it with someone who needs the encouragement.

6

Family and Friends

What you do in your house is worth as much as if you did it up in heaven for our Lord God.

MARTIN LUTHER

Peace in society depends upon peace in the family.

ST AUGUSTINE

Family and friendships are two of the greatest facilitators of happiness.

JOHN C. MAXWELL

Peace and war begin at home. If we truly want peace in the world, let us begin by loving one another in our own families. If we want to spread joy, we need for every family to have joy.

MOTHER TERESA

Friendships are discovered rather than made.

HARRIET BEECHER STOWE

Name one thing you are grateful for regarding at least 5 people in your family.

Describe a memory you cherish most with a loved one.

What are you most thankful for about your relationship with God?

Name a loved one who is no longer here whom you are thankful for. Why?

Promises from God's Word

Two are better than one, because they have a good return for their labor: If either of them falls down, one can help the other up. But pity anyone who falls and has no one to help them up.

ECCLESIASTES 4:9–10 NIV

Bear one another's burdens, and so fulfill the law of Christ.

GALATIANS 6:2 NKJV

If we walk in the light as He is in the light, we have fellowship with one another, and the blood of Jesus Christ His Son cleanses us from all sin.

1 JOHN 1:7 NKJV

Just as our bodies have many parts and each part has a special function, so it is with Christ's body. We are many parts of one body, and we all belong to each other.

ROMANS 12:4–5 NLT

Behold, how good and pleasant it is when brothers dwell in unity!

PSALM 133:1 ESV

I ALWAYS
thank my God
FOR YOU
BECAUSE OF HIS
grace
given
YOU IN
Christ Jesus.
1 CORINTHIANS 1:4 NIV

Do you have a mentor you appreciate who encourages you? How did that person change your life, and how can you show your appreciation?

Name one thing you are grateful for regarding at least 3 people outside your immediate family.

Name one friend you are grateful for. Why?

Prayer Time

Father God,

Thank You for the people You've placed in my life, for the relationships we have, for the way they shape me, challenge me, and help me grow. May I never take these relationships for granted, but always seek to nurture and cherish them with Your love.

Lord, I'm most grateful for the most important relationship anybody could have—my relationship with You. Thank You for Your love, which never fails and is always steadfast.

In Jesus' name, Amen.

Gratitude Challenge

Organize a picnic with loved ones that you can all enjoy together.

7

The Gift of Salvation

God's salvation does not come in response to a changed life. A changed life comes in response to the salvation, offered as a free gift.

TIMOTHY KELLER

Salvation is the free gift of God by Jesus Christ, and the work of it is supernatural. It is done by the Lord Himself, and He has power to do it, however weak, no, however dead in sin, the sinner may be.

CHARLES SPURGEON

The power of God unto salvation is not our passion for God, but the passion He has exhibited toward us sinners by sending His own Son to redeem us.

MICHAEL HORTON

Christ sets us free by the power of His Spirit; then He maintains our freedom as we learn to live from day to day in the power of that Spirit.

BETH MOORE

Salvation is accomplished by the almighty power of the Triune God. The Father chose a people, the Son died for them, the Holy Spirit makes Christ's death effective by bringing the elect to faith and repentance, thereby causing them to willingly obey the gospel. The entire process (election, redemption, regeneration) is the work of God and is by grace alone.

LORAINE BOETTNER

Reflect on the first time someone shared the Good News of Jesus with you. Where was it? How old were you? Who shared it with you? How did you feel?

Who can you share your faith with in your own life?

Read Matthew 28:1–8. Reflect on the empty tomb and what it means for those who are children of God.

You are a new creation in Christ! What does it mean for you to have a new identity in Christ, to no longer be held captive by your past sins?

Promises from God's Word

God saved you by His grace when you believed. And you can't take credit for this; it is a gift from God. Salvation is not a reward for the good things we have done, so none of us can boast about it.

EPHESIANS 2:8–9 NLT

Come, let us sing for joy to the LORD; let us shout aloud to the Rock of our salvation. Let us come before Him with thanksgiving and extol Him with music and song.

PSALM 95:1–2 NIV

If you confess with your mouth the Lord Jesus and believe in your heart that God has raised Him from the dead, you will be saved.

ROMANS 10:9 NKJV

"For this is how God loved the world: He gave His one and only Son, so that everyone who believes in Him will not perish but have eternal life."

JOHN 3:16 NLT

He has delivered us from the domain of darkness and transferred us to the kingdom of His beloved Son, in whom we have redemption, the forgiveness of sins.

COLOSSIANS 1:13–14 ESV

Praise
THE LORD,
my soul, &
FORGET NOT ALL HIS BENEFITS—
who forgives
ALL YOUR SINS
AND HEALS ALL YOUR DISEASES,
WHO REDEEMS YOUR LIFE
FROM THE PIT
AND CROWNS YOU
WITH love & compassion.
PSALM 103:2-4 NIV

Write down the lyrics of your favorite worship song, thanking God for His gift of salvation.

According to John 14:2–3, Jesus is preparing a place for us in eternity. What do you imagine that would be like?

How can you show gratitude to God for His great gift of salvation?

Prayer Time

Write a prayer of thanksgiving for salvation and freedom from sin.

Gratitude Challenge

Share the Good News of God's salvation with at least 1 person.

8

Health, Healing and Restoration

I venture to say that the greatest earthly blessing that God can give to any of us is health, with the exception of sickness. Sickness has frequently been of more use to the saints of God than health has…Trials drive us to the realities of religion.

CHARLES SPURGEON

Health is a good thing; but sickness is far better, if it leads us to God.

J. C. RYLE

Pray, always pray; when sickness wastes thy frame, prayer brings the healing power of Jesus' name.

A. B. SIMPSON

My heart, which is so full to overflowing, has often been solaced and refreshed by music when sick and weary.

MARTIN LUTHER

Our Heavenly Healer often has to hurt us in order to heal us. We sometimes fail to recognize His mighty love in this, yet we are firmly held always in the Everlasting Arms.

ELISABETH ELLIOT

Think about a time when you faced a challenge related to your health and overcame it. Write about the experience, including what you learned and how you grew from it.

Has there been a situation in your life where God has healed you or a family member in an unexpected way? Describe the situation and how it made you feel.

How does focusing on gratitude impact your healing process?

Promises from God's Word

Praise the LORD, my soul, and forget not all His benefits—who forgives all your sins and heals all your diseases.

PSALM 103:2–3 NIV

My son, give attention to my words; incline your ear to my sayings. Do not let them depart from your eyes; keep them in the midst of your heart; for they are life to those who find them, and health to all their flesh.

PROVERBS 4:20–22 NKJV

Is anyone among you sick? Let him call for the elders of the church, and let them pray over him, anointing him with oil in the name of the Lord. And the prayer of faith will save the one who is sick, and the Lord will raise him up.

JAMES 5:14–15 ESV

Don't be impressed with your own wisdom. Instead, fear the LORD and turn away from evil. Then you will have healing for your body and strength for your bones.

PROVERBS 3:7–8 NLT

"Come to Me, all you who are weary and burdened, and I will give you rest. Take My yoke upon you and learn from Me, for I am gentle and humble in heart, and you will find rest for your souls."

MATTHEW 11:28–29 NIV

"'BUT I WILL
restore
YOU TO health
AND HEAL YOUR
WOUNDS,'
declares
the LORD."
JEREMIAH 30:17 NIV

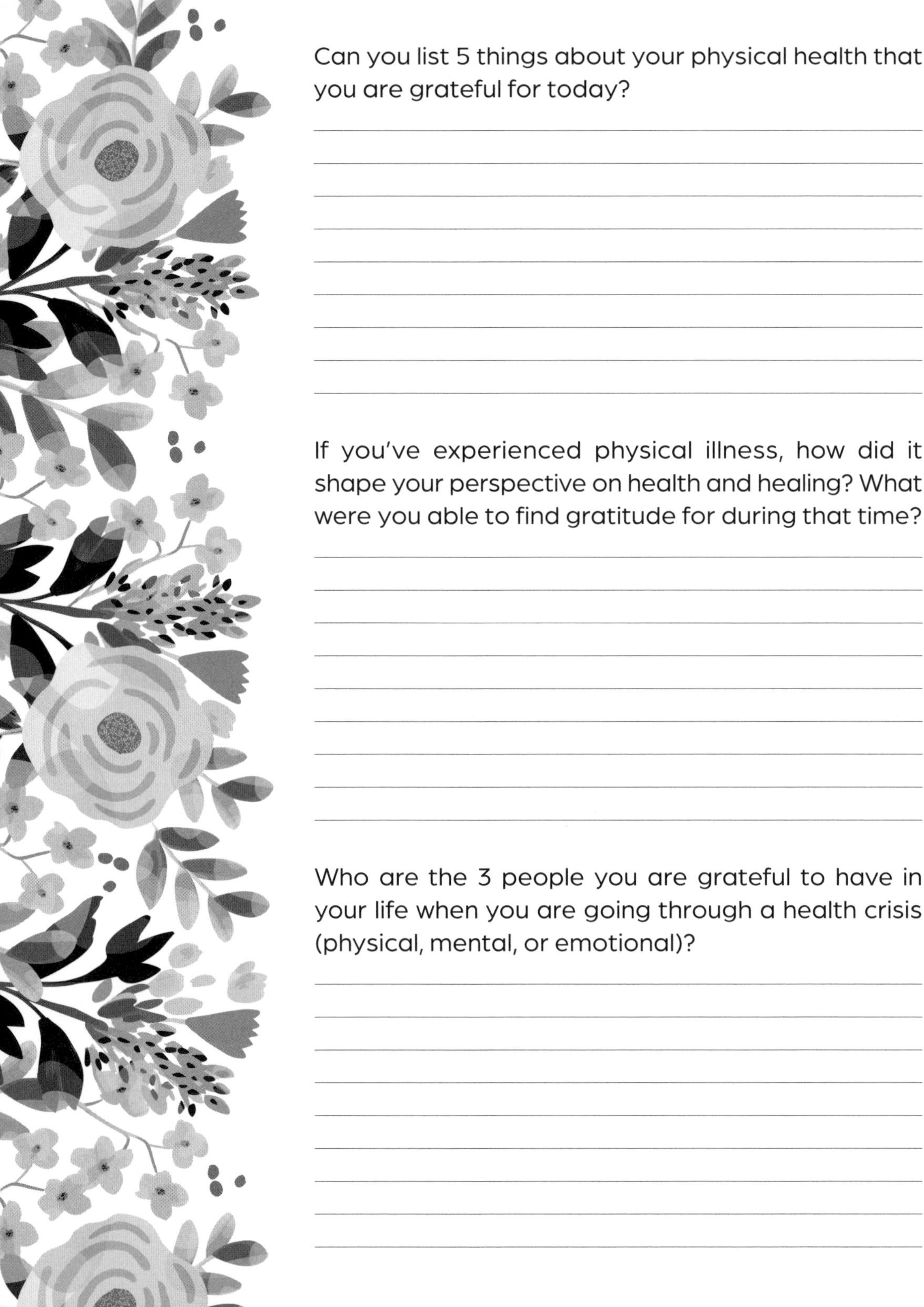

Can you list 5 things about your physical health that you are grateful for today?

If you've experienced physical illness, how did it shape your perspective on health and healing? What were you able to find gratitude for during that time?

Who are the 3 people you are grateful to have in your life when you are going through a health crisis (physical, mental, or emotional)?

Prayer Time

Heavenly Father,

You are the Great Physician in whom we can trust in times of sickness and health. Thank You for that.

Lord, in James 5:14–16, You promise that if we pray in faith, there will be healing. This is such a comfort, Father. And yet we also know that healing is not always within Your will. When this is the case, please give us the understanding, acceptance, and comfort that is needed.

Remind us, Lord, of Your promise that in heaven there will be no more sickness and suffering. Thank You that we can entrust our health to You, knowing that You know best and will not let us down.

In Jesus' name, Amen.

Gratitude Challenge

Write thank you notes to 3 people who supported you during a health crisis (physical, mental, or emotional) and hand-deliver them if possible.

9

God's Daily Mercies

God's mercy is so great that you may sooner drain the sea of its water, or deprive the sun of its light, or make space too narrow, than diminish the great mercy of God.

CHARLES SPURGEON

The mercy of God is an all-embracing mercy and it breaks down the barriers that man erects.

ALISTAIR BEGG

Our worst days are never so bad that you are beyond the reach of God's grace. And your best days are never so good that you are beyond the need of God's grace.

JERRY BRIDGES

Grace is the voice that calls us to change and then gives us the power to pull it off. It is God's mercy and grace that save us and shape us into the people He wants us to be, and we are to live in a constant state of gratitude for that incredible mercy.

MAX LUCADO

Maybe it's only those who've made such chaos of their lives who can understand the heights and depths of God's mercy.

FRANCINE RIVERS

Reflect on how God's mercies are new every morning.

What does God's grace mean to you personally?

How can you show more grace to the people around you?

Have you ever felt unworthy of God's grace? Why?

Promises from God's Word

But He said to me, "My grace is sufficient for you, for My power is made perfect in weakness." Therefore I will boast all the more gladly of my weaknesses, so that the power of Christ may rest upon me.

2 CORINTHIANS 12:9 ESV

But by the grace of God I am what I am, and His grace to me was not without effect. No, I worked harder than all of them—yet not I, but the grace of God that was with me.

1 CORINTHIANS 15:10 NIV

So let us come boldly to the throne of our gracious God. There we will receive His mercy, and we will find grace to help us when we need it most.

HEBREWS 4:16 NLT

May the God of all grace, who called us to His eternal glory by Christ Jesus, after you have suffered a while, perfect, establish, strengthen, and settle you.

1 PETER 5:10 NKJV

For the grace of God has appeared that offers salvation to all people. It teaches us to say "No" to ungodliness and worldly passions, and to live self-controlled, upright and godly lives in this present age.

TITUS 2:11–12 NIV

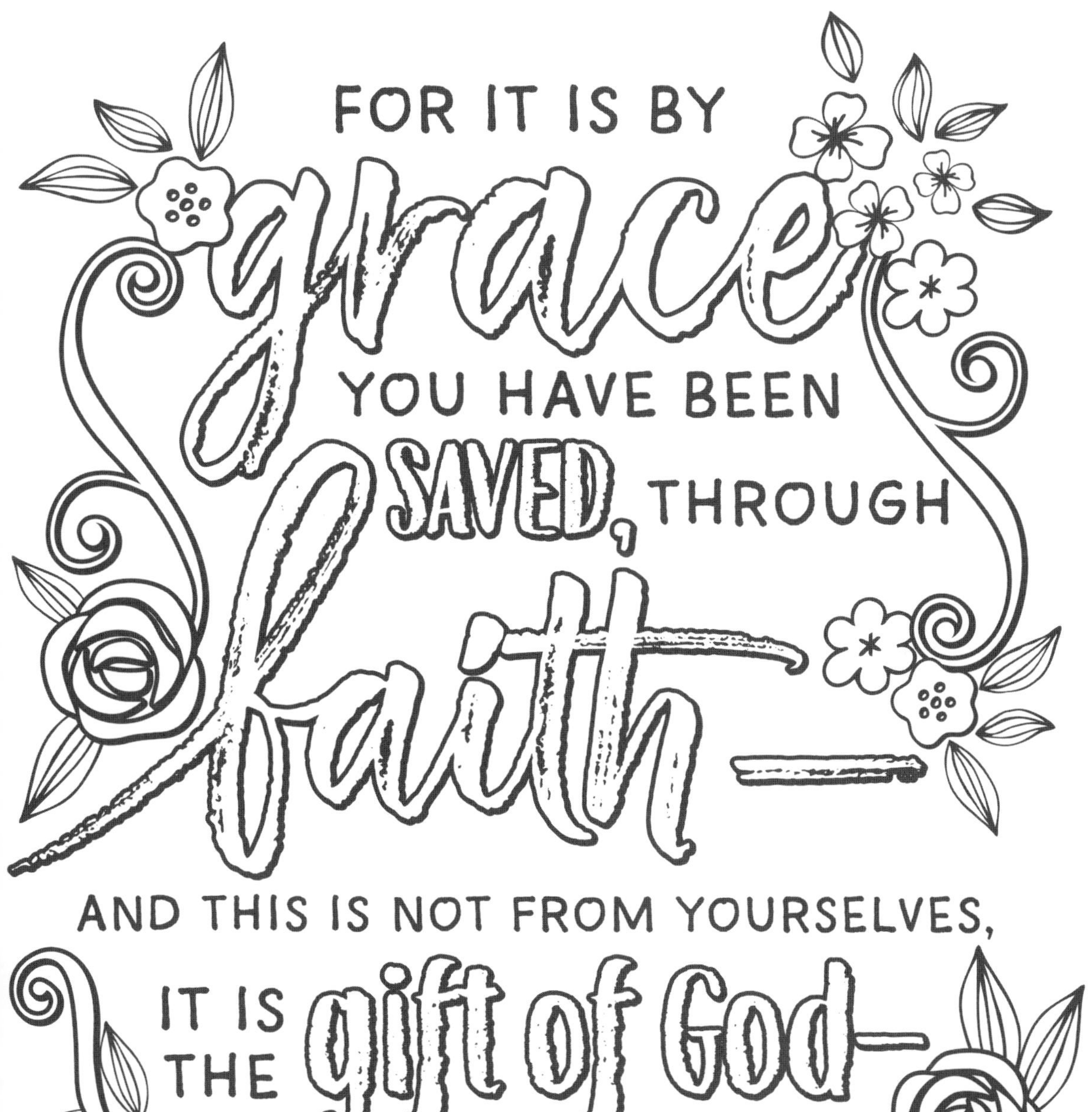

NOT BY WORKS,
SO THAT NO ONE CAN BOAST.

EPHESIANS 2:8-9 NIV

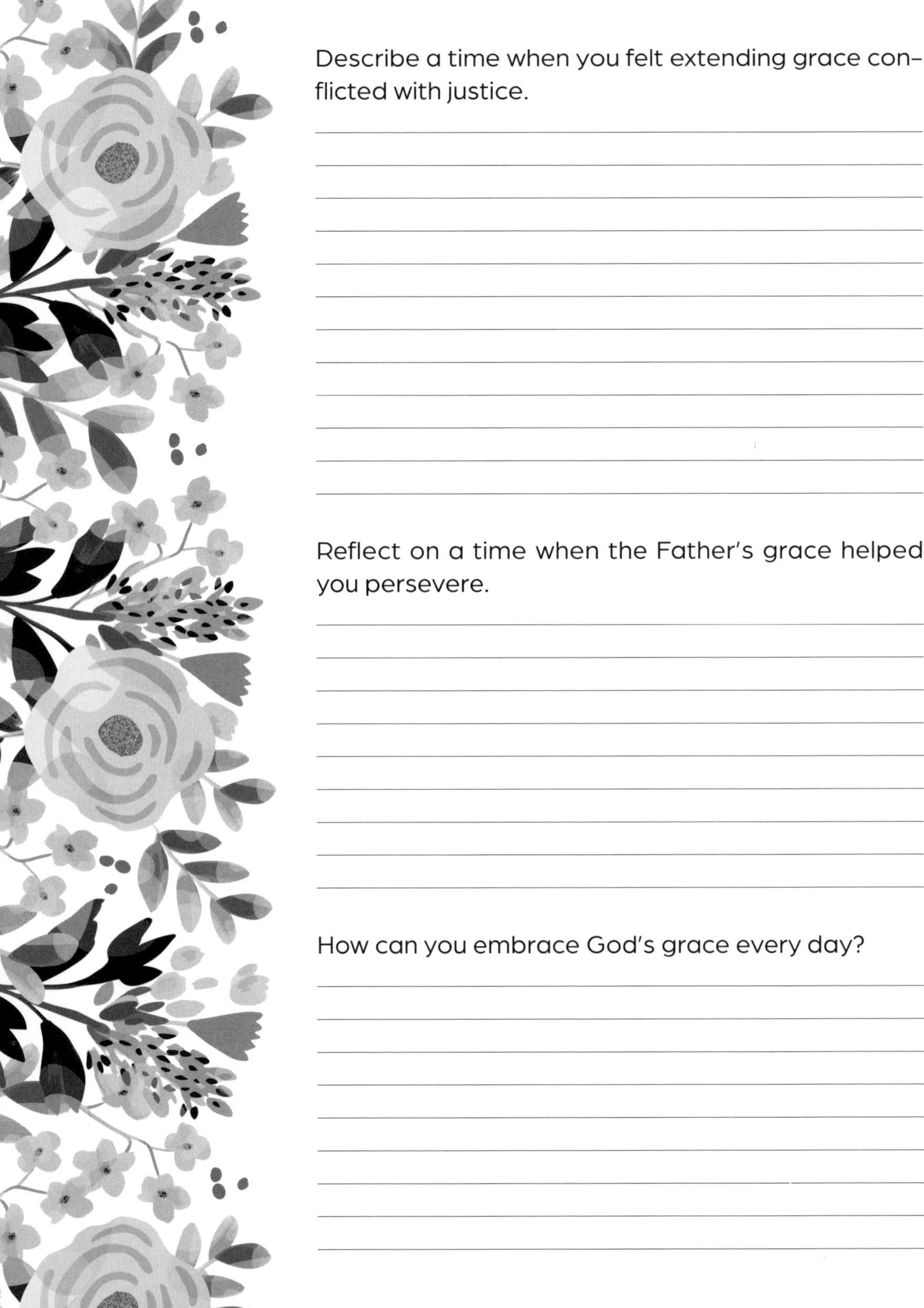

Describe a time when you felt extending grace conflicted with justice.

Reflect on a time when the Father's grace helped you persevere.

How can you embrace God's grace every day?

Prayer Time

Write a prayer thanking God for His daily mercies.

Gratitude Challenge

For the following week, write down one mercy God has shown you every day and thank Him for it.

10

God's Provision

Rest assured that the Lord, who daily provides for the millions of fish in the sea and the myriads of birds in the air, will not suffer His own children to perish for lack of the things of this life.

CHARLES SPURGEON

God has promised to supply our needs. What we don't have now, we don't need now.

ELISABETH ELLIOT

God meets daily needs daily. Not weekly or annually. He will give you what you need when it is needed.

MAX LUCADO

When God gives you a mission, He also gives you everything you need to fulfill that mission.

ELIZABETH GEORGE

God does not give us everything we want, but He does fulfill His promises, leading us along the best and straightest paths to Himself.

DIETRICH BONHOEFFER

God's work done in God's way will never lack God's supply.

HUDSON TAYLOR

Recall a time when you were in need. How did God provide for your needs, and how did you show your gratitude?

List your 5 most important needs that God is currently meeting.

Can you name 3 worship songs you can sing when you want to thank God for His provision?

List 3 things you enjoyed today that somebody else might not have. How can you thank God for providing those basic necessities you often take for granted?

Promises from God's Word

And my God shall supply all your need according to His riches in glory by Christ Jesus.

PHILIPPIANS 4:19 NKJV

All creatures look to You to give them their food at the proper time. When You give it to them, they gather it up; when You open Your hand, they are satisfied with good things.

PSALM 104:27–28 NIV

"Give us this day our daily bread."

MATTHEW 6:11 ESV

And God will generously provide all you need. Then you will always have everything you need and plenty left over to share with others.

2 CORINTHIANS 9:8 NLT

The eyes of all look to You in hope; You give them their food as they need it. When You open Your hand, You satisfy the hunger and thirst of every living thing.

PSALM 145:15–16 NLT

THE LORD
IS MY
shepherd
I LACK
NOTHING.
PSALM 23:1 NIV

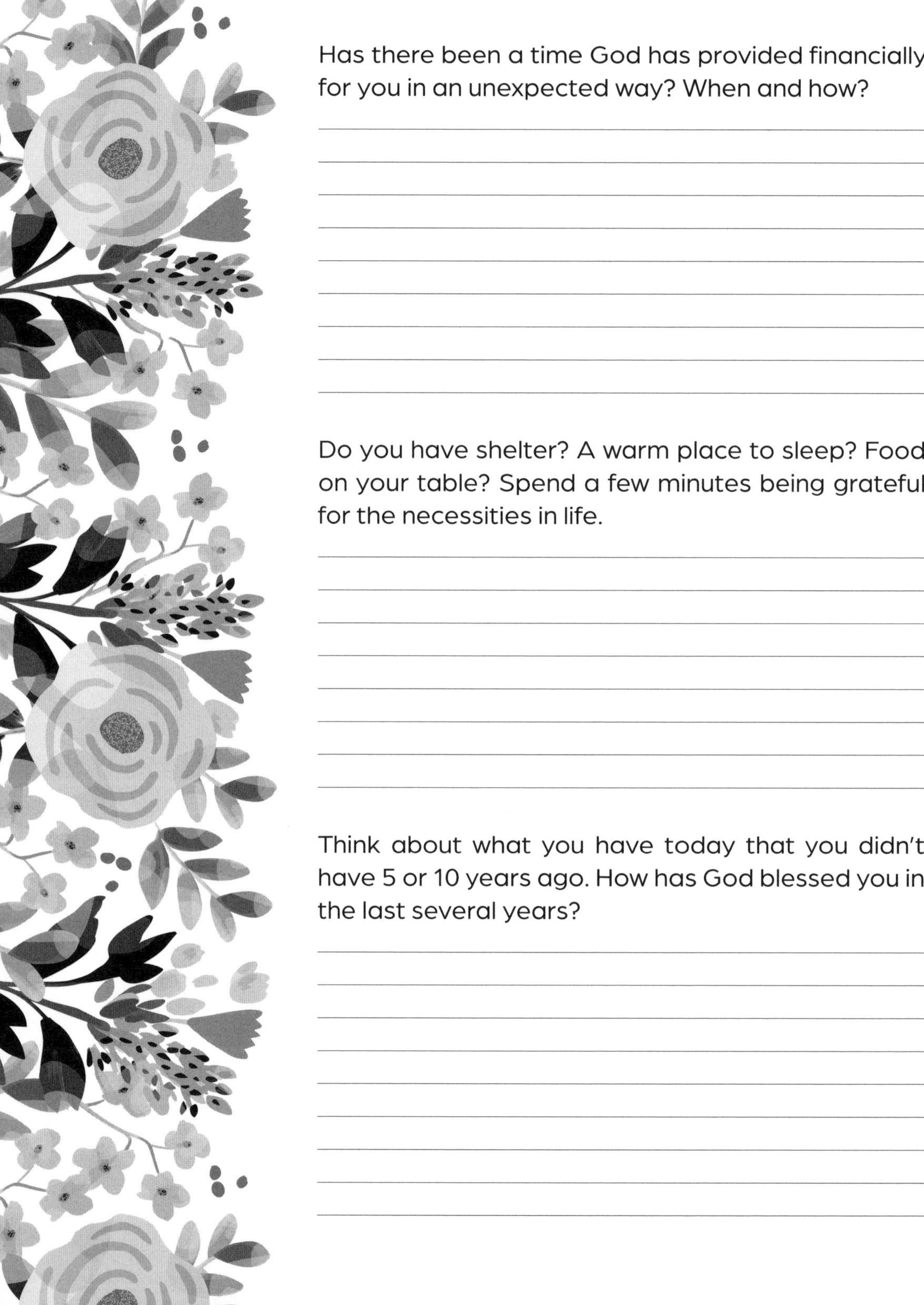

Has there been a time God has provided financially for you in an unexpected way? When and how?

Do you have shelter? A warm place to sleep? Food on your table? Spend a few minutes being grateful for the necessities in life.

Think about what you have today that you didn't have 5 or 10 years ago. How has God blessed you in the last several years?

Prayer Time

Father God,

There is no provider greater than You. Your Word, Lord, reminds us not to worry about the needs of daily life—food and clothes—because You are faithful to provide. Thank You for meeting all of my needs—physical, emotional, and spiritual. I am grateful for Your constant care and provision.

In Jesus' name, Amen.

Gratitude Challenge

Donate or offer your time to an organization that helps people in need.

Daily Gratitude

What is your favorite Bible verse? What makes it meaningful to you?

What is something from each of your senses you are grateful for each day?

Sight ______ Touch ______

Smell ______ Sound ______

Taste ______

What are the character traits of God you appreciate the most? Why?

Name 3 everyday objects that you are grateful for.

What is something in your home that brings you great joy and why?

Think of something you often take for granted (clean water, free wifi, etc.) and write about why you're thankful for it.

What is one personal strength you're grateful for and why?

Reflect on your daily routine. What part of the day brings you the most joy and why?

List your favorite...

Quiet time space

Hobby

Book

Sport

Hymn

Snack

Movie

List 3 tangible things that make your daily life better and that you are grateful for.

What moment in your past are you most grateful for today?

List 3 things that made you smile today.

Name a person you are thankful for who shaped who you are today.

What is the best compliment you've received?

11

Thankfulness in Trials

God will not permit any troubles to come upon us, unless He has a specific plan by which great blessing can come out of the difficulty.

PETER MARSHALL

Circumstances may appear to wreck our lives and God's plans, but God is not helpless among the ruins. God's love is still working. He comes in and takes the calamity and uses it victoriously, working out His wonderful plan of love.

ERIC LIDDELL

Does God guarantee the absence of struggle and the abundance of strength? Not in this life. But He does pledge to reweave your pain for a higher purpose.

MAX LUCADO

It is great to be faced with the impossible, for nothing is impossible if one is meant to do it. Wisdom will be given, and strength. When the Lord leads, He always strengthens.

AMY CARMICHAEL

Struggles will be an integral part of life as long as we're alive, so don't let yourself believe that your challenges mean that God has rejected you. Instead, focus on the fact that He is the God who cares deeply in the midst of the challenges.

FRANCINE RIVERS

Write down the Scripture verse you hold on to when you are experiencing a challenge or going through a trial.

Have you ever seen the benefit in a challenge you overcame? Describe the challenge and the benefit thereof.

If you are currently going through a trial, what do you think God wants you to learn from it?

Looking back on your hardest trials, how can you express gratitude for the way they've shaped who you are today?

Promises from God's Word

I lift up my eyes to the hills. From where does my help come? My help comes from the LORD, who made heaven and earth.

PSALM 121:1–2 ESV

"When you pass through the waters, I will be with you; and when you pass through the rivers, they will not sweep over you. When you walk through the fire, you will not be burned; the flames will not set you ablaze."

ISAIAH 43:2 NIV

Dear brothers and sisters, when troubles of any kind come your way, consider it an opportunity for great joy. For you know that when your faith is tested, your endurance has a chance to grow. So let it grow, for when your endurance is fully developed, you will be perfect and complete, needing nothing.

JAMES 1:2–4 NLT

Praise be to the God and Father of our Lord Jesus Christ, the Father of compassion and the God of all comfort, who comforts us in all our troubles, so that we can comfort those in any trouble with the comfort we ourselves receive from God.

2 CORINTHIANS 1:3–4 NIV

We know that all things work together for good to those who love God, to those who are the called according to His purpose.

ROMANS 8:28 NKJV

GOD IS OUR
refuge
& strength,
AN EVER-PRESENT
HELP IN TROUBLE.
PSALM 46:1 NIV

Write down the names of people who supported you while you were going through a trial and how they supported you.

How do you think God can use a trial you are going through now to help strengthen someone else?

How can embracing gratitude for past struggles help you face future trials with more confidence?

Prayer Time

Write a prayer thanking God for the challenges you face and the opportunity they bring for spiritual growth.

Gratitude Challenge

List 3 ways you can support and comfort somebody you know who is going through a tough time, and then do it.

12 Acts of Kindness

There is no reward equal to that of doing the most good to the most people in the most need.

EVANGELINE BOOTH

Be the living expression of God's kindness; kindness in your eyes, kindness in your face, kindness in your smile, kindness in your warm greetings. We are all but His instruments who do our little bit and pass by. I believe that the way in which an act of kindness is done is as important as the action itself.

MOTHER TERESA

Kindness begets kindness.

PROVERB

True gratitude or thankfulness to God for His kindness to us, arises from a foundation laid before, of love to God for what He is in Himself; whereas a natural gratitude has no such antecedent foundation. The gracious stirrings of grateful affection to God, for kindness received, always are from a stock of love already in the heart, established in the first place on other grounds, viz. God's own excellency.

JONATHAN EDWARDS

Have you ever noticed how much of Christ's life was spent in doing kind things?

HENRY DRUMMOND

Describe a time when somebody did something unexpectedly for you that you appreciated.

Why do you think kindness is one of the fruit of the Spirit (Gal. 5:22–23)?

Reflect on how God blessed you through a small act of kindness.

How can you show acts of kindness to someone?

Promises from God's Word

Whenever we have the opportunity, we should do good to everyone—especially to those in the family of faith.

GALATIANS 6:10 NLT

Make sure that nobody pays back wrong for wrong, but always strive to do what is good for each other and for everyone else.

1 THESSALONIANS 5:15 NIV

The generous will prosper; those who refresh others will themselves be refreshed.

PROVERBS 11:25 NLT

Whoever has this world's goods, and sees his brother in need, and shuts up his heart from him, how does the love of God abide in him? My little children, let us not love in word or in tongue, but in deed and in truth.

1 JOHN 3:17–18 NKJV

"And the King will answer them, 'Truly, I say to you, as you did it to one of the least of these My brothers, you did it to Me.'"

MATTHEW 25:40 ESV

DO NOT FORGET TO DO

good and to share

WITH OTHERS,

FOR WITH SUCH SACRIFICES

God is pleased.

HEBREWS 13:16 NIV

What is the best gift you've ever received, and how did you show your appreciation?

List specific ways God has cared for or blessed you lately, even in quiet or surprising moments.

Write about a kind act you were able to do for some-one else. How did it feel to serve in love?

Prayer Time

Lord,

Thank You for all the graces that we receive so undeservedly from Your hand. Thank You, Father, for people who assist and support us when we least expect it.

Make us aware of the needs of others so that we can also lend a helping hand without expecting anything in return.

Amen.

Gratitude Challenge

Put together a care package for someone in need and deliver it to them anonymously.

13 God's Forgiveness

Most laws condemn the soul and pronounce sentence. The result of the law of my God is perfect. It condemns but forgives. It restores—more than abundantly—what it takes away.

JIM ELLIOT

Nothing in the Christian life is more important than forgiveness—our forgiveness of others and God's forgiveness of us.

JOHN F. MACARTHUR

God's forgiveness extends to the worst offenders and to anyone who wishes to receive it—not because of who we are, but because of who He is.

CHARLES SWINDOLL

God's forgiveness is not just a casual statement; it is the complete blotting out of all the dirt and degradation of our past, present and future.

BILLY GRAHAM

Our sins have been put away. To use the language of the Scriptures... they are completely removed, put behind God's back, blotted out, remembered no more, and hurled into the depths of the sea.

JERRY BRIDGES

As a child of God, your sins were washed away by the price Jesus paid for you. How do you feel when you think about what Jesus had to endure so you could be completely forgiven?

Can you recall a time when you experienced God's forgiveness and how you showed your gratitude?

Can you share something in your life you haven't forgiven yourself for?

What Scripture verse reminds you most of God's forgiveness?

Promises from God's Word

He does not punish us for all our sins; He does not deal harshly with us, as we deserve. For His unfailing love toward those who fear Him is as great as the height of the heavens above the earth. He has removed our sins as far from us as the east is from the west.

PSALM 103:10–12 NLT

If we confess our sins, He is faithful and just to forgive us our sins and to cleanse us from all unrighteousness.

1 JOHN 1:9 ESV

In Him we have redemption through His blood, the forgiveness of sins, according to the riches of His grace.

EPHESIANS 1:7 NKJV

If You, LORD, kept a record of sins, Lord, who could stand? But with You there is forgiveness, so that we can, with reverence, serve You.

PSALM 130:3–4 NIV

Where is another God like You, who pardons the guilt of the remnant, overlooking the sins of His special people? You will not stay angry with Your people forever, because You delight in showing unfailing love. Once again You will have compassion on us. You will trample our sins under Your feet and throw them into the depths of the ocean!

MICAH 7:18–19 NLT

"Blessed
ARE THOSE WHOSE
TRANSGRESSIONS ARE
forgiven,
WHOSE SINS
ARE COVERED.
Blessed is the one
WHOSE SIN THE LORD
WILL NEVER COUNT
AGAINST THEM."
ROMANS 4:7-8 NIV

God is a God of second chances. Can you name 3 Bible characters whose sins were forgiven a second or third time?

Who or what do you need to forgive in your life?

What does forgiveness look like?

How can you show gratitude for God's forgiveness in your daily life?

Prayer Time

Read Isaiah 1:18 and write a prayer thanking and praising God for His forgiveness.

Gratitude Challenge

Write a letter to somebody you need to forgive. Even if you don't send them the letter, the important thing is that you forgive them in your heart.

Peace in the Storm

We want Christ to hurry and calm the storm. He wants us to find Him in the midst of it first.

BETH MOORE

God cannot give us a happiness and peace apart from Himself, because it is not there. There is no such thing.

C. S. LEWIS

Restlessness and impatience change nothing except our peace and joy. Peace does not dwell in outward things, but in the heart prepared to wait trustfully and quietly on Him who has all things safely in His hands.

ELISABETH ELLIOT

Jesus made it possible for us to have the peace that passes all understanding—the kind that carries us, stabilizes us, grounds us, and keeps us from slipping.

STORMIE OMARTIAN

Peace does not dwell in outward things but within the soul; we may preserve it in the midst of the bitterest pain, if our will remains firm and submissive. Peace in this life springs from acquiescence to, not an exemption from, suffering.

FRANÇOIS FÉNELON

Recall a Scripture verse that brings you peace.

Read Philippians 4:7 and reflect on a time when God's peace surpassed your understanding.

If you are currently experiencing a storm, list things you can thank God for, even though you don't feel peace?

What storm are you experiencing now, and how can you invite God's peace into it today?

Promises from God's Word

Let the peace that comes from Christ rule in your hearts. For as members of one body you are called to live in peace. And always be thankful.

COLOSSIANS 3:15 NLT

"I am leaving you with a gift—peace of mind and heart. And the peace I give is a gift the world cannot give. So don't be troubled or afraid."

JOHN 14:27 NLT

Grace to you and peace from God the Father and our Lord Jesus Christ, who gave Himself for our sins, that He might deliver us from this present evil age, according to the will of our God and Father, to whom be glory forever and ever. Amen.

GALATIANS 1:3–5 NKJV

Great peace have those who love your law, and nothing can make them stumble.

PSALM 119:165 NIV

The peace of God, which transcends all understanding, will guard your hearts and your minds in Christ Jesus.

PHILIPPIANS 4:7 NIV

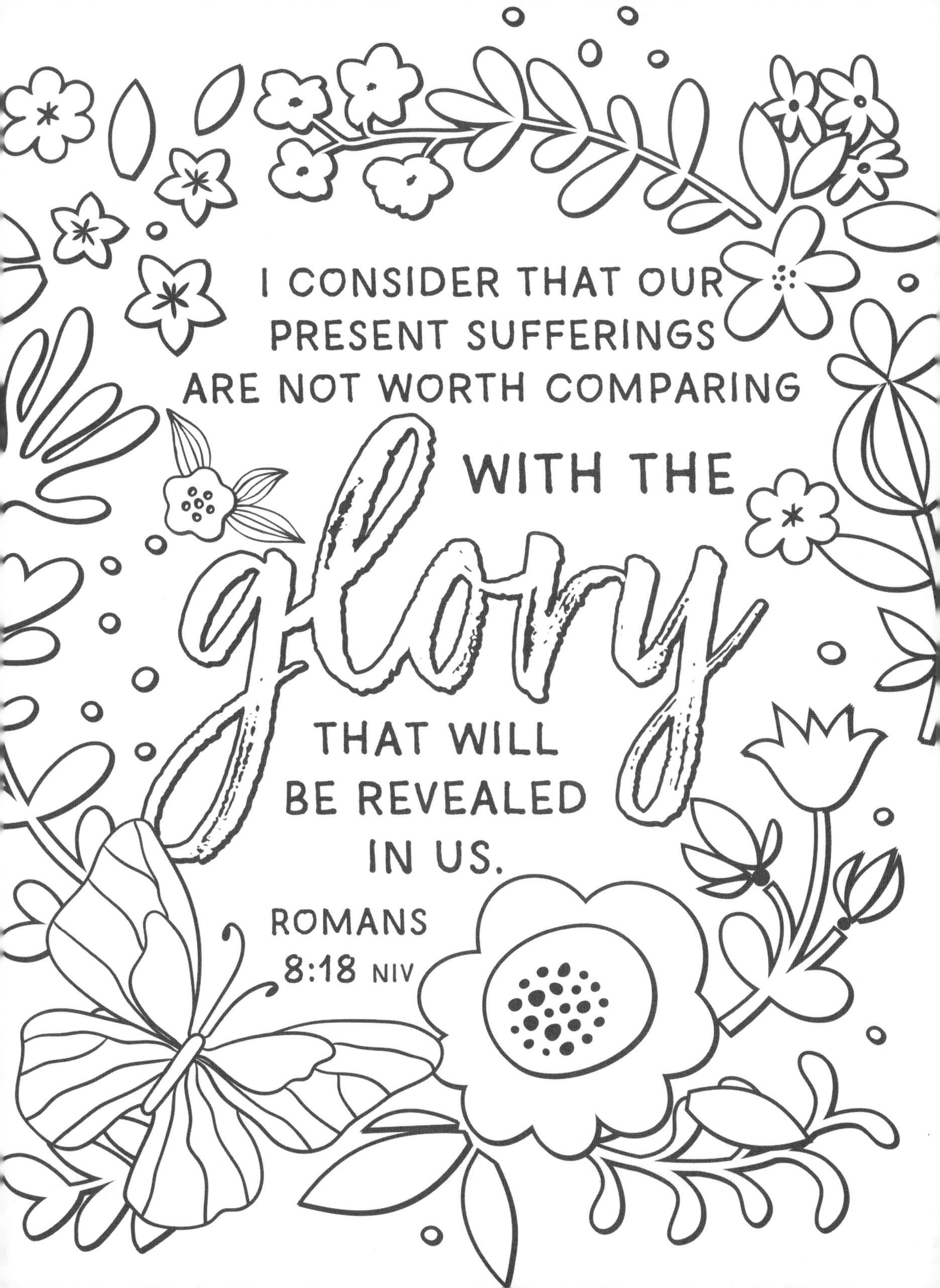
I CONSIDER THAT OUR
PRESENT SUFFERINGS
ARE NOT WORTH COMPARING
WITH THE
glory
THAT WILL
BE REVEALED
IN US.
ROMANS
8:18 NIV

What small moments of calm has God given you in the middle of big storms that you are grateful for?

Why do you think peace is a fruit of the Spirit (Gal. 5:22–23)?

List 3 people you are grateful for who supported you during a storm?

Prayer Time

God,

Grant me the serenity to accept the things I cannot change, courage to change the things I can, and wisdom to know the difference.

Amen.

Gratitude Challenge

Every morning for 7 days, write a Scripture verse that reminds you of God's peace. Then write one thing you are grateful for that day.

God's Timing

He is not only a God of perfect time, but of perfect timing.

BETH MOORE

Never forget that God isn't bound by time the way we are. We see only the present moment; God sees everything. We see only part of what He is doing; He sees it all.

BILLY GRAHAM

There are no "ifs" in God's kingdom. His timing is perfect. His will is our hiding place. Lord Jesus, keep me in Your will! Don't let me go mad by poking about outside it.

CORRIE TEN BOOM

Mercy may seem slow, but it is sure. The Lord in unfailing wisdom has appointed a time for the outgoings of His gracious power, and God's time is the best time.

CHARLES SPURGEON

Waiting on God requires the willingness to bear uncertainty, to carry within oneself the unanswered question, lifting the heart to God about it whenever it intrudes upon one's thoughts.

ELISABETH ELLIOT

According to Ecclesiastes, there is a time and season for everything. What season are you currently in?

Can you describe a time when you felt frustrated with God's timing?

Can you describe a time when you felt thankful for God's timing?

Reflect on a moment when you made time for something or someone that you are now grateful for. Why are you grateful for it now?

Promises from God's Word

He has made everything beautiful in its time. Also, He has put eternity into man's heart, yet so that he cannot find out what God has done from the beginning to the end.

ECCLESIASTES 3:11 ESV

But when the set time had fully come, God sent His Son, born of a woman, born under the law.

GALATIANS 4:4 NIV

Wait patiently for the LORD. Be brave and courageous. Yes, wait patiently for the LORD.

PSALM 27:14 NLT

The Lord is not slow in keeping His promise, as some understand slowness. Instead He is patient with you, not wanting anyone to perish, but everyone to come to repentance.

2 PETER 3:9 NIV

When we were still without strength, in due time Christ died for the ungodly.

ROMANS 5:6 NKJV

ISAIAH 60:22 NLT
"AT THE
right time,
I, THE LORD,
WILL make it
happen."

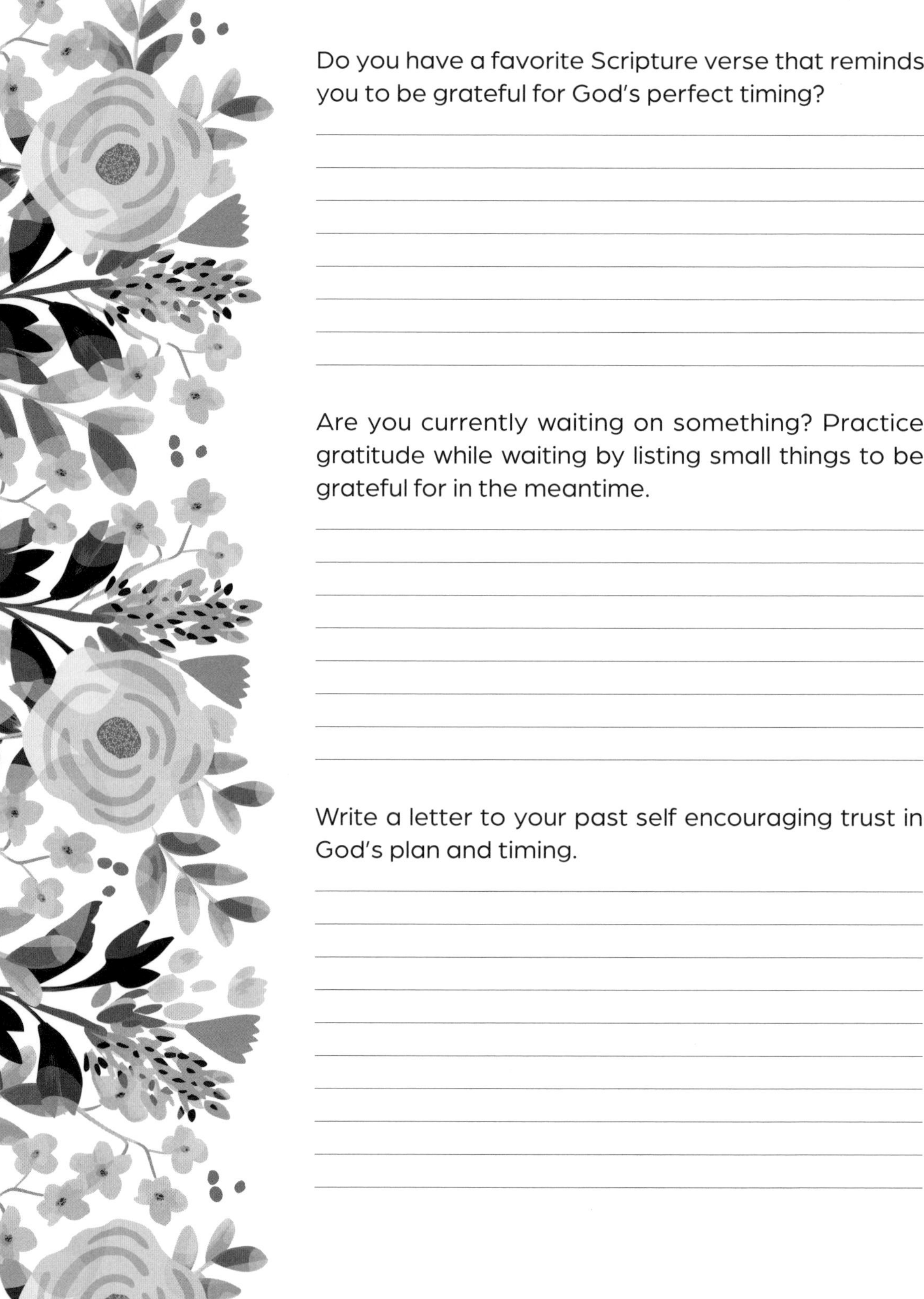

Do you have a favorite Scripture verse that reminds you to be grateful for God's perfect timing?

Are you currently waiting on something? Practice gratitude while waiting by listing small things to be grateful for in the meantime.

Write a letter to your past self encouraging trust in God's plan and timing.

Prayer Time

Recall a time when God's timing protected you from something and write a prayer to thank God for it.

Gratitude Challenge

Give someone the gift of your time. Make special arrangements to spend quality time with a loved one.

16

A Time for Work

Every occupation has its own honor before God. Ordinary work is a divine vocation or calling. In our daily work no matter how important or mundane we serve God by serving the neighbor and we also participate in God's ongoing providence for the human race.

MARTIN LUTHER

The essence of our work as humans must be that it is done in conscious reliance on God's power, and in conscious quest of God's pattern of excellence, and in deliberate aim to reflect God's glory.

JOHN PIPER

The way to worship God while the daylight lasts is to work; the service of God, the only "divine service," is the helping of our fellows.

GEORGE MACDONALD

Work is a blessing. God has so arranged the world that work is necessary, and He gives us hands and strength to do it. The enjoyment of leisure would be nothing if we had only leisure. It is the joy of work well done that enables us to enjoy rest.

ELISABETH ELLIOT

Christ never was in a hurry. There was no rushing forward, no anticipating, no fretting over what might be. Each day's duties were done as each day brought them, and the rest was left with God.

MARY SLESSOR

What do you appreciate most about your work?

Do you think the Bible commandment, "Six days you shall labor and do all your work, but the seventh day is the Sabbath of the LORD your God. In it you shall do no work" (Exodus 20:9–10 NKJV), only refers to a job that pays a salary or does it refer to any kind of work you do? Explain.

How are you using the talents and strengths God has given you in your workplace? How can you thank God for them?

Do you have a colleague who has a positive impact on your day or career? What did they do, and how did you show your appreciation?

Promises from God's Word

People should eat and drink and enjoy the fruits of their labor, for these are gifts from God.

ECCLESIASTES 3:13 NLT

Whatever you do, do it heartily, as to the Lord and not to men, knowing that from the Lord you will receive the reward of the inheritance; for you serve the Lord Christ.

COLOSSIANS 3:23–24 NKJV

Let the favor of the Lord our God be upon us, and establish the work of our hands upon us; yes, establish the work of our hands!

PSALM 90:17 ESV

The LORD God took the man and put him in the Garden of Eden to work it and take care of it.

GENESIS 2:15 NIV

Who can find a virtuous and capable wife? She is more precious than rubies...Reward her for all she has done. Let her deeds publicly declare her praise.

PROVERBS 31:10, 31 NLT

NEVER BE LACKING
in zeal,
BUT KEEP YOUR
spiritual fervor,
serving
THE LORD.
ROMANS 12:11 NIV

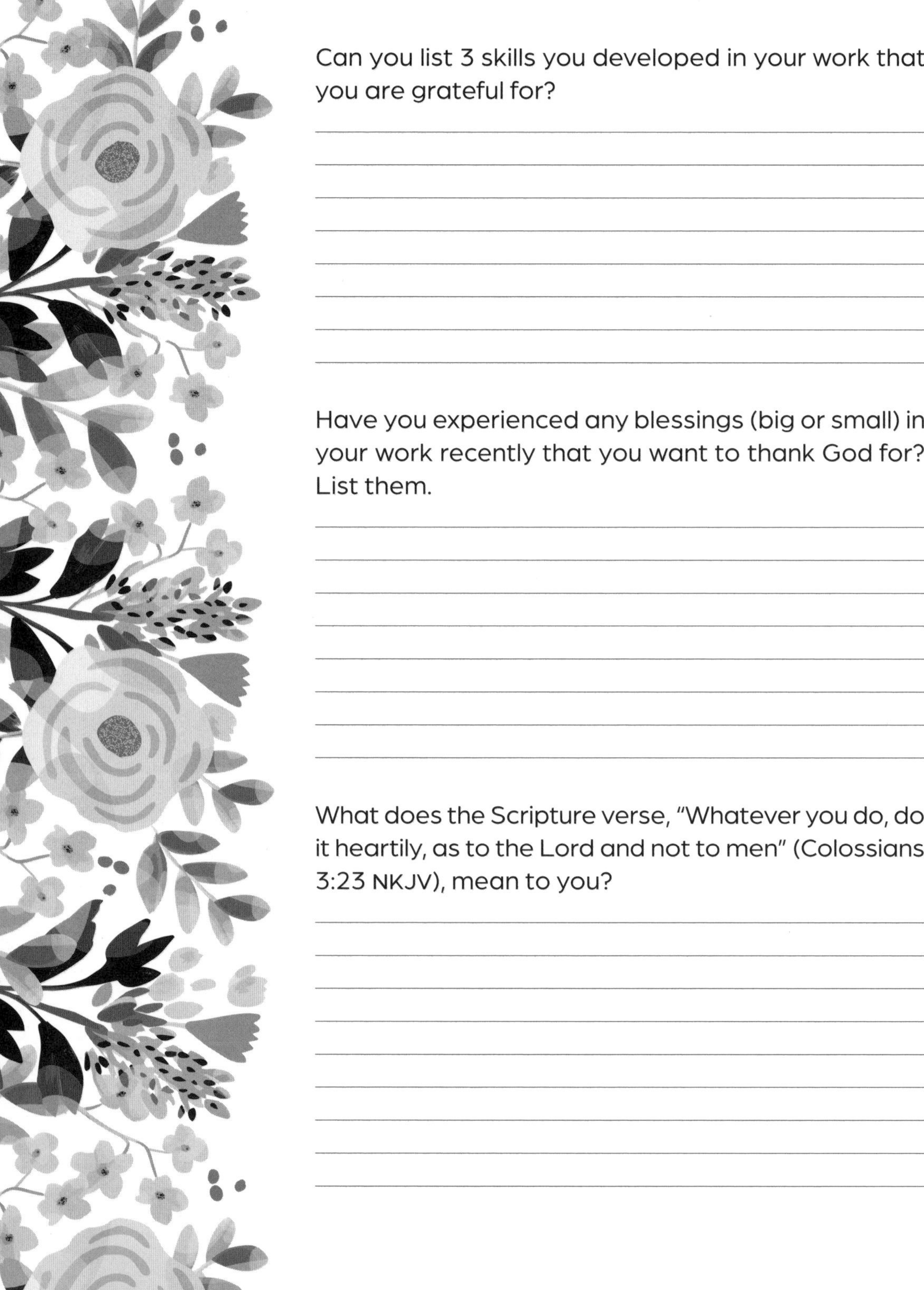

Can you list 3 skills you developed in your work that you are grateful for?

Have you experienced any blessings (big or small) in your work recently that you want to thank God for? List them.

What does the Scripture verse, "Whatever you do, do it heartily, as to the Lord and not to men" (Colossians 3:23 NKJV), mean to you?

Prayer Time

Heavenly Father,

You created humanity to work, as You commanded Adam and Eve in the Garden of Eden. This calling is divine—it is a gift and a means for me to glorify You. Thank You for providing me with a purpose.

Lord, please guide me in understanding how my work aligns with Your greater plan for my life. Help me to be more enthusiastic in my efforts and grateful for the opportunity to dedicate all that I do to You. Amen.

Gratitude Challenge

Invite someone who helped you accomplish your work or supported you in your work for coffee to say thank you.

Time to Rest

In place of our exhaustion and spiritual fatigue, God will give us rest. All He asks is that we come to Him…that we spend a while thinking about Him, meditating on Him, talking to Him, listening in silence, occupying ourselves with Him—totally and thoroughly lost in the hiding place of His presence.

CHARLES SWINDOLL

God directs that each seventh day be kept as a day of rest from the labors of the previous six…The day is to be kept "holy"—that is, it is to be used for honoring God the Creator by worship, as well as for refreshing human creatures by the break from their otherwise unending toil.

J. I. PACKER

Rest is a weapon given to us by God. The enemy hates it because he wants us to be stressed and occupied.

ELISABETH ELLIOT

God knows we need rest, and one of the reasons He established the Sabbath was to give us rest…God's plan was to use the Sabbath to turn our hearts and minds toward Him. In other words, He wants us to set aside one day of the week as a special time of worship and reflection on God's Word.

BILLY GRAHAM

Recall a time when you felt weary and burdened, and God gave you rest.

What do you like to do for relaxation?

"You have six days each week for your ordinary work, but the seventh day must be a Sabbath day of complete rest, a holy day dedicated to the LORD" (Exodus 31:15 NLT). Do you have one day a week that you dedicate to the Lord? How do you usually spend that day?

Recall a Scripture promise about rest that has spoken to you and how God has fulfilled that promise in your life.

Promises from God's Word

On the seventh day God ended His work which He had done, and He rested on the seventh day from all His work which He had done. Then God blessed the seventh day and sanctified it, because in it He rested from all His work which God had created and made.

GENESIS 2:2–3 NKJV

Then, because so many people were coming and going that they did not even have a chance to eat, He said to them, "Come with Me by yourselves to a quiet place and get some rest."

MARK 6:31 NIV

So there is a special rest still waiting for the people of God. For all who have entered into God's rest have rested from their labors, just as God did after creating the world.

HEBREWS 4:9–10 NLT

And He said, "My presence will go with you, and I will give you rest."

EXODUS 33:14 ESV

He lets me rest in green meadows; He leads me beside peaceful streams. He renews my strength.

PSALM 23:2–3 NLT

"Come
to Me,
ALL YOU WHO ARE
WEARY AND BURDENED,
and I will
give you
rest."
MATTHEW 11:28-29 NIV

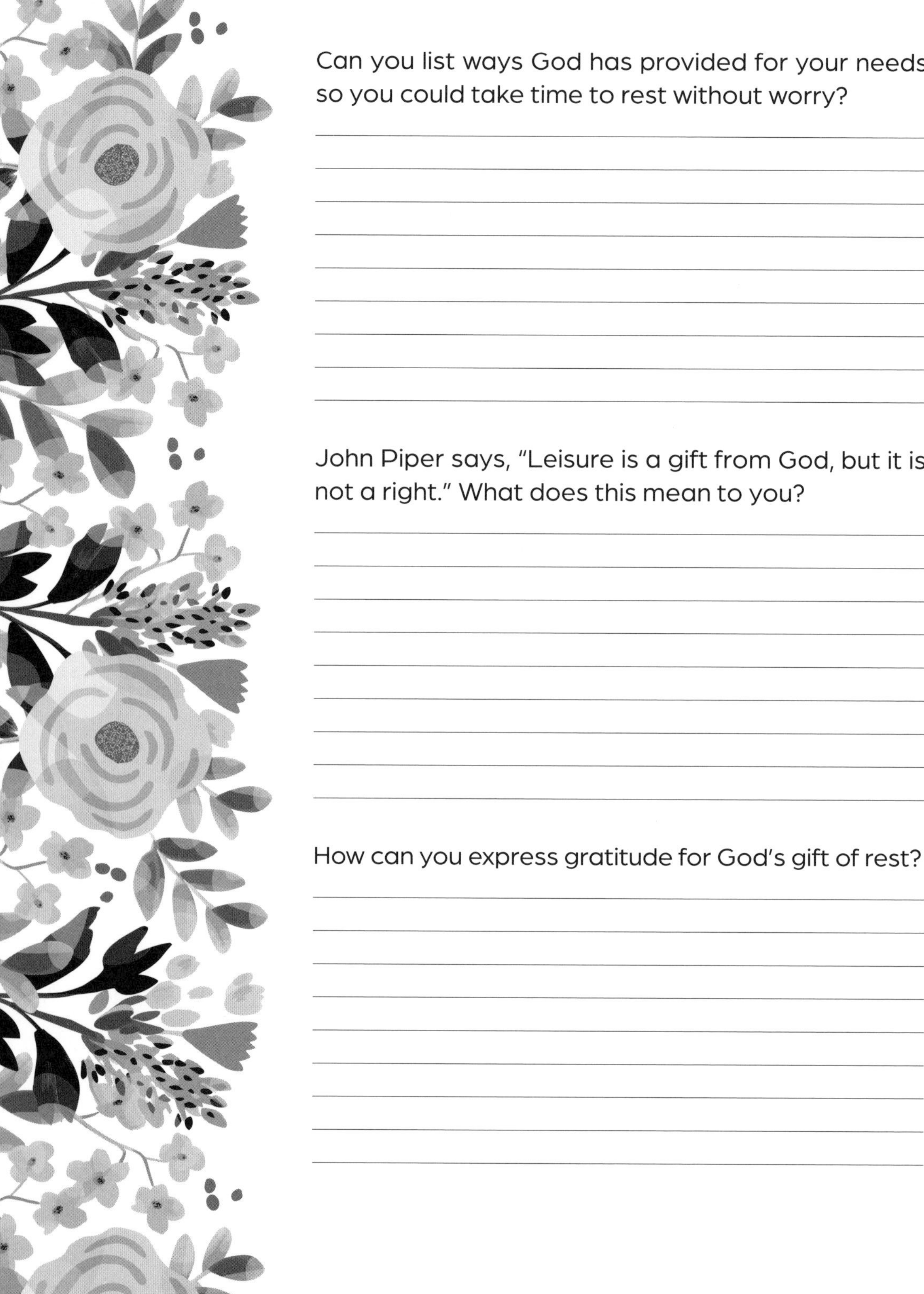

Can you list ways God has provided for your needs so you could take time to rest without worry?

John Piper says, "Leisure is a gift from God, but it is not a right." What does this mean to you?

How can you express gratitude for God's gift of rest?

Prayer Time

Write a prayer of thanks to God for the rest you recently experienced.

Gratitude Challenge

For 1 month, do 1 chore or task every week for a loved one so they can use that time to rest.

God's Protection

To be sure, God shall call you, and us, only at the hour that God has chosen. Until that hour, which lies in God's hand alone, we shall be protected even in the greatest danger; and from our gratitude for such protection ever new readiness surely arises for the final call.

DIETRICH BONHOEFFER

The safest place in all the world is in the will of God, and the safest protection in all the world is the name of God.

WARREN WIERSBE

We must always keep in mind all legitimate authority is from God, and is given for protection, provision, and peace.

JOHN BEVERE

God will be your shield. He will protect you from harm. In Him, you are always safe.

UNKNOWN

In Jesus Christ on the Cross, there is refuge; there is safety; there is shelter; and all the power of sin upon our track cannot reach us when we have taken shelter under the Cross that atones for our sins.

A. C. DIXON

Can you recall a time when you experienced God's protection in a very real way? What happened, and how did you express your gratitude?

Write down your favorite Scripture verse that reminds you of the heavenly Father's protection.

What does the Scripture verse, "If God is for us, who can be against us?" (Romans 8:31 NIV) mean to you?

Protection is not only physical. Can you recall a time when God protected you spiritually in the past month?

Promises from God's Word

He shall cover you with His feathers, and under His wings you shall take refuge; His truth shall be your shield and buckler.

PSALM 91:4 NKJV

"No weapon that is fashioned against you shall succeed, and you shall refute every tongue that rises against you in judgment. This is the heritage of the servants of the LORD and their vindication from Me, declares the LORD."

ISAIAH 54:17 ESV

What, then, shall we say in response to these things? If God is for us, who can be against us?

ROMANS 8:31 NIV

But the Lord is faithful; He will strengthen you and guard you from the evil one.

2 THESSALONIANS 3:3 NLT

"Let the beloved of the LORD rest secure in Him, for He shields him all day long, and the one the LORD loves rests between His shoulders."

DEUTERONOMY 33:12 NIV

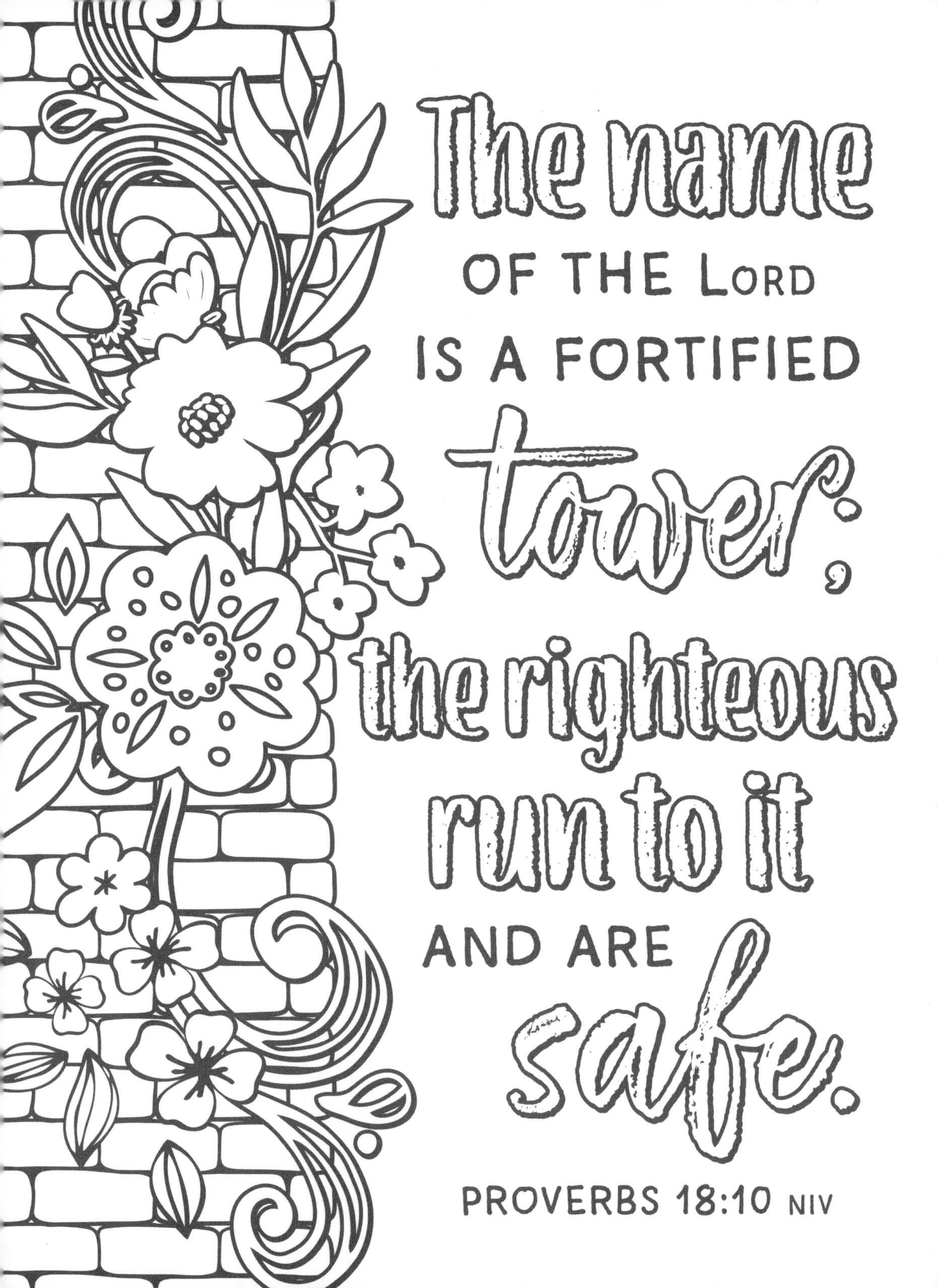
The name
of the Lord
is a fortified
tower;
the righteous
run to it
and are
safe.
PROVERBS 18:10 NIV

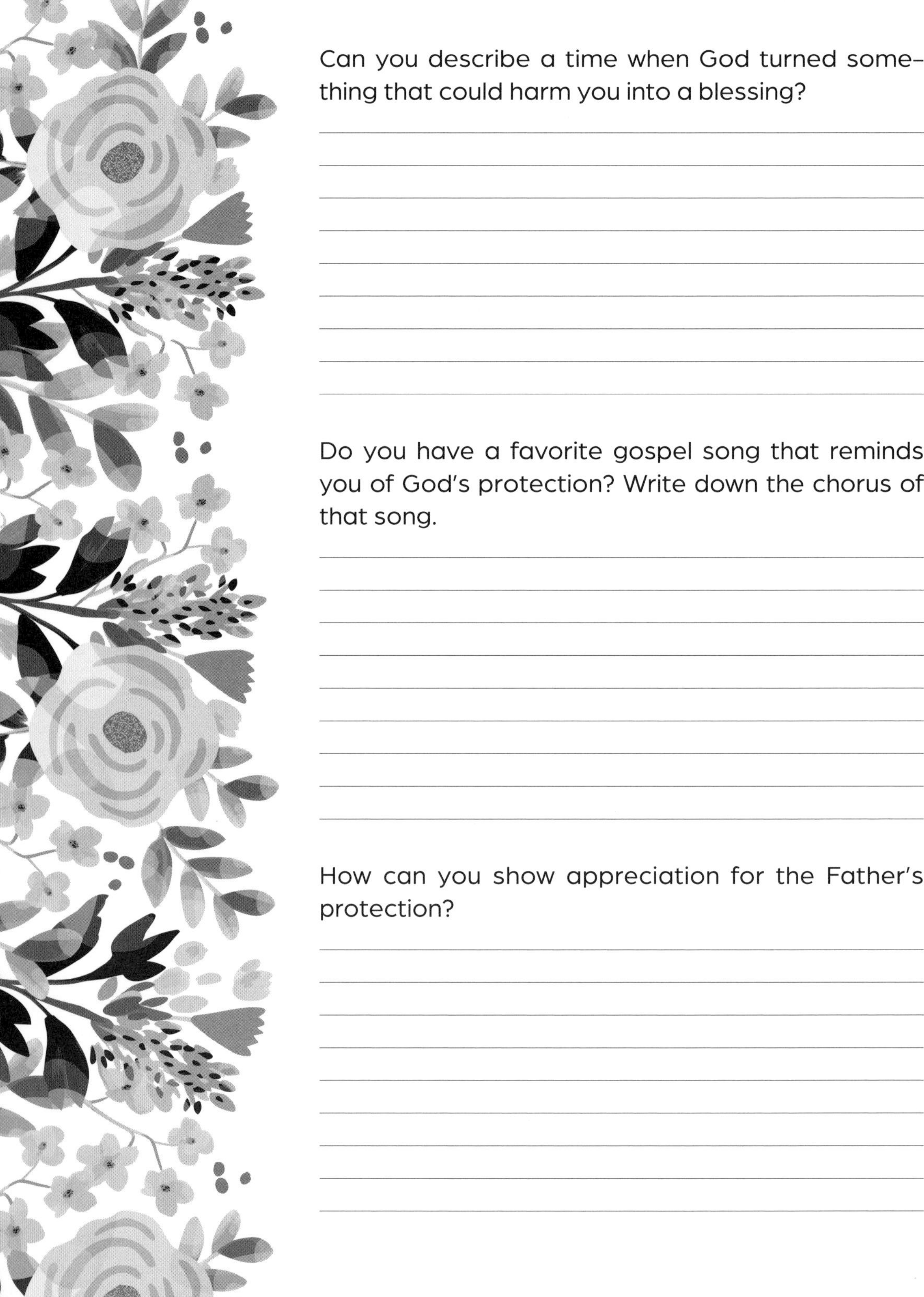

Can you describe a time when God turned something that could harm you into a blessing?

Do you have a favorite gospel song that reminds you of God's protection? Write down the chorus of that song.

How can you show appreciation for the Father's protection?

Prayer Time

Father God,

You are truly my refuge and strength in whom I can trust. Thank You for protecting me physically, emotionally, and spiritually.

Amen.

Gratitude Challenge

Choose a Scripture verse or quote regarding God's protection. Write it on a few cards, and give it to loved ones to remind them of God's protection.

19

Hope in Christ

Faith looks back and draws courage; hope looks ahead and keeps desire alive.

JOHN ELDREDGE

Hope is like an anchor. Our hope in Christ stabilizes us in the storms of life, but unlike an anchor, it does not hold us back.

CHARLES SWINDOLL

Our hope in Christ for the future is the mainspring and the mainstay of our joy down here today.

CHARLES SPURGEON

Many things are possible for the person who has hope. Even more is possible for the person who has faith. And still more is possible for the person who knows how to love. But everything is possible for the person who practices all three virtues.

BROTHER LAWRENCE

Optimism is a wish without warrant; Christian hope is a certainty, guaranteed by God Himself. Optimism reflects ignorance as to whether good things will ever actually come. Christian hope expresses knowledge that every day of his life, and every moment beyond it, the believer can say with truth, on the basis of God's own commitment, that the best is yet to come.

J. I. PACKER

Read Isaiah 40:31. What does it mean for you to hope in the Lord?

List 3 songs that express something about the hope we have in Jesus.

Can you recall a time when God showed you hope when you needed it? How did you show your gratitude?

Give an example of a Scripture verse for each of the following types of hope: hope in salvation, hope as a virtue, and hope as an expectation of future good.

Promises from God's Word

I pray that God, the source of hope, will fill you completely with joy and peace because you trust in Him. Then you will overflow with confident hope through the power of the Holy Spirit.

ROMANS 15:13 NLT

Praise be to the God and Father of our Lord Jesus Christ! In His great mercy He has given us new birth into a living hope through the resurrection of Jesus Christ from the dead.

1 PETER 1:3 NIV

But since we belong to the day, let us be sober, having put on the breastplate of faith and love, and for a helmet the hope of salvation.

1 THESSALONIANS 5:8 ESV

While we wait for the blessed hope—the appearing of the glory of our great God and Savior, Jesus Christ…

TITUS 2:13 NIV

I pray that your hearts will be flooded with light so that you can understand the confident hope He has given to those He called—His holy people who are His rich and glorious inheritance.

EPHESIANS 1:18 NLT

WE HAVE THIS
HOPE
AS AN
anchor
FOR THE
soul,
firm and secure.
HEBREWS 6:19 NIV

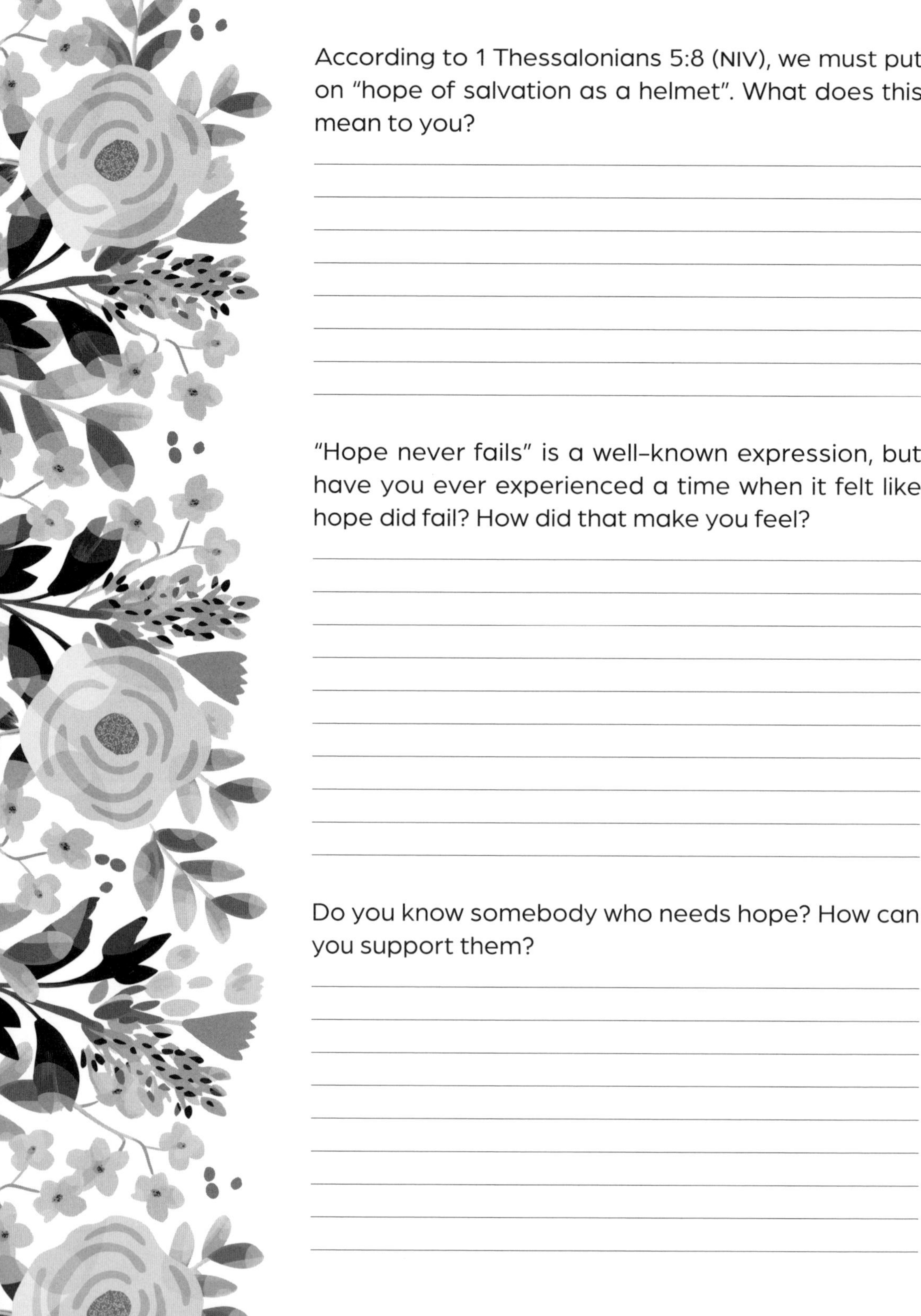

According to 1 Thessalonians 5:8 (NIV), we must put on "hope of salvation as a helmet". What does this mean to you?

"Hope never fails" is a well-known expression, but have you ever experienced a time when it felt like hope did fail? How did that make you feel?

Do you know somebody who needs hope? How can you support them?

Prayer Time

Write a prayer of praise to God for the hope you have in Him.

Gratitude Challenge

Download an image of one Scripture promise on hope and set it as your phone's wallpaper for one month.

20

The Word of God

The success of God's Word in our lives is linked intrinsically to our application of its truth.

JONI EARECKSON TADA

The Bible was not given for our information but for our transformation.

DWIGHT L. MOODY

Beloved, surrender wholeheartedly to Jesus Christ, who loves you. As you drink from the deep well of Scripture, the Lord will refresh you and cleanse you, mold you and re-create you through His Living Word. For the Bible is the very breath of God, giving life eternal to those who seek Him.

FRANCINE RIVERS

I have done nothing; the Word has done and accomplished everything...I let the Word do its work!

MARTIN LUTHER

The Bible is the Word of God in such a way that when the Bible speaks, God speaks.

B. B. WARFIELD

Why are you grateful for God's Word?

Recall a time when you found true guidance in God's Word in a specific situation.

What role does Scripture play in your daily life, and how are you grateful for its guidance and presence?

Do you have a spiritual mentor who helps you answer questions you have about God's Word? How do they inspire you to read your Bible more?

Promises from God's Word

"Heaven and earth will pass away, but My words will never pass away."

MATTHEW 24:35 NIV

"For as the rain and the snow come down from heaven and do not return there but water the earth, making it bring forth and sprout, giving seed to the sower and bread to the eater, so shall My word be that goes out from My mouth; it shall not return to Me empty, but it shall accomplish that which I purpose, and shall succeed in the thing for which I sent it."

ISAIAH 55:10–11 ESV

All Scripture is inspired by God and is useful to teach us what is true and to make us realize what is wrong in our lives. It corrects us when we are wrong and teaches us to do what is right. God uses it to prepare and equip His people to do every good work.

2 TIMOTHY 3:16–17 NLT

For the word of God is alive and powerful. It is sharper than the sharpest two-edged sword.

HEBREWS 4:12 NLT

For the word of the LORD is right, and all His work is done in truth.

PSALM 33:4 NKJV

Your word
IS A
lamp
FOR MY FEET,
a light
ON MY
path.
PSALM 119:105 NIV

Reflect on your favorite Bible verse and how it keeps you anchored in the promises of God.

How do you memorize Scripture verses?

Read 2 Timothy 3:16–17. Reflect on why you need to treasure God's Word.

Prayer Time

Heavenly Father,

All Scripture is inspired by You, and what a remarkable Book it is—a collection of 66 individual books, written by more than 40 authors over more than 1,600 years.

Thank You for providing us with this wonderful guide to direct our steps, teach us what is true and right, and correct us when we go astray.

I am grateful for the way You reveal Yourself to us through Your Word, allowing us to get to know You better. It is such a joy to spend time in Your Word daily and to have my soul nourished by it. Amen.

Gratitude Challenge

Give a Bible to someone who needs one, or donate to a Bible Society.

We would like to hear from you.
Please send your comments about this journal
to comments@christianart.co.za